The trip

T
T

There was something the matter with the clan.
Everyone felt gloomy.
They were all fed up because there was nothing to do.
Hilda was angry with Big Ben because he had upset a big pan of food she was cooking for dinner.
Now everyone would have to go without their dinner.
She was so angry that she hit Big Ben with her wooden spoon.
Tosh lost his temper because the pan had landed on his foot.
Now his best boots were all messy.
He called Big Ben a silly fool.
Big Ben went off in a sulk.
The clan Macfuzz had never felt so grumpy.
Everyone just got crosser and crosser.
In the end, some of the little ones went to see if Jock could help.

Jock was in the garden at the back of his house, chopping up some wood.
He put the chopper down and sat on a rock to do a bit of thinking.
'Let's all go off on a day-trip,' he said at last.
The little ones went zooming off to ask the rest of the clan.
Everyone sat up.
They were all interested.
'We could have a picnic,' said Don.
'We could put lots of things to eat and drink into a big picnic hamper.
Then we could carry it up to the top of the hills.'
'Yes, yes,' said the little ones.
'Can we go now?'

crisps
pop
jam

The chief of the clan, called Macfuzz the buzz, stood up and said that this was a jolly good plan.
They would set off on the very next day.
Hilda said that the little ones could help to cook some extra food for the picnic.
Windbag took out his bagpipes, and Don did a little jig.
Suddenly, everybody felt much better.
The next day, everything was ready.
The picnic hamper was full to the top with lots of food and drink.
It was so full that Ben had to carry it, because he was the biggest.
The clan went across the River Mac and up into the trees.
It was a sunny day.
They were very glad to get to the top of the first big hill.
By now they all felt hot and sticky.
They sat down on the grass to cool off.
But the clan were not at the top yet.
There was a bigger hill to get up first.
They set off again.

At last they were all standing at the top of the very biggest hill.
Hilda put a big, blue cloth down on the grass and began to lift the food out of the picnic hamper.
She took out apples and oranges, drinks of fizzy pop, little pots of jam and butter, lots of buns, packets of crisps, a big dish of jelly and a set of spoons, and lots more.
There was plenty for everybody.
Before long, everyone was full up.

The afternoon sun was hotter than ever.
Macfuzz the buzz was dropping off to sleep.
The little ones were too hot to play.
Soon they were nodding off too.
In the end, everyone was snoozing.
But not Big Ben.
He was not sleepy at all.
He stood up and went across to a big, brown rock that stuck out from the top of the hill.
Big Ben got on top of it.
Now he could look down into the next glen.

B

This glen was horrid.
It was dull and gloomy.
It was full of ugly cliffs and jagged rocks.
Big Ben could see a twisty, crooked path going down into the glen.
It went into a very thick clump of prickly bushes.
Then the crooked path went zig-zagging past some nasty, jagged rocks.
The path ended at a smooth, still pool.
This pool was green and stagnant.
Next to the pool there was an ugly, rocky cliff.
At the foot of the cliff there stood a bent and twisted tree.
Next to the tree, Big Ben could see a black and gloomy cave.
By now, the rest of the clan had come to see what Ben was looking at.
'I would love to go and have a look down there,' said Ben.
'Will someone come with me?'
Nobody said a word.

The
Glen
of Gloom

Big Ben set off down the crooked path.
'Stop!' Black Angus called out.
Big Ben stopped.
'Just come here and read this,' said Black Angus, and he nodded at some funny letters that were cut into the bottom of the big rock.
Big Ben went across to read the words.
'It's called "The Glen of Gloom",' he said.

Black Angus felt a shiver running down his back.
'Yes,' he said.
'It looks very spooky to me.
If you go down there we will all be sorry.
I think that something very, very wicked lives in that glen.
We must not bother it.
If we do, it will creep and slither out of its nasty den.
Then it will hunt us down and trap us.
It will never give up.'

But nothing was going to stop Big Ben.
'What a lot of silly rubbish!' he said, and back down the path he went.
Windbag ran after him.
'I will come with you,' he panted.
The rest of the clan could see the two fuzzbuzzes going down the zig-zag path.
But nobody would go after them.
'No good will come of this,' said Black Angus sadly. 'No good at all!'

B
Ben

By now, Big Ben and Windbag were well down the crooked path.
Soon they had come to the clump of prickly bushes.
These bushes were drooping across the path, shutting out the sun.
The two fuzzbuzzes crept in.
They felt as if they were going into a long and gloomy tunnel.
'Hurry up!' panted Windbag.
'It's creepy in here!'

Then suddenly, the prickly bushes began to jerk and twist.
Clinging together, the two fuzzbuzzes had to bob and duck as roots and twigs shot out at them.
Windbag's bonnet went spinning off.
Within seconds, the prickly twigs were ripping it to shreds.
The two fuzzbuzzes began to run.
But the twigs from the bushes were

flicking and jabbing
pricking and grabbing
pushing and nipping
rushing and ripping
looping and snatching
swooping and scratching.

'Come on,' panted Ben.
'We must run faster.'
At long last the two fuzzbuzzes got to the end of the tunnel.
Suddenly, the bushes stopped jerking.
Everything was still again.

The two fuzzbuzzes sat down on a rock for a rest.
Windbag was very unhappy.
His kilt was in tatters.
There was blood on his hands where the prickly twigs had cut his skin.
He was so upset that he began to stammer.
'I am n-n-not going on,' he said to Ben.
'The b-b-bushes w-were out to get us.
What will happen n-n-next?'
Big Ben could see that Windbag felt very jumpy.
He felt sorry for Windbag, but he was going to see the rest of the glen if it was the last thing he ever did.
He stood up and patted Windbag on the back.
'You sit here for a bit,' he said.
'I will go on.'
Then Big Ben set off down the path again.

The path began to zig-zag in and out of the big, jagged rocks.
By now, Big Ben could see the muddy banks of the still green pool.
But as he went on, something very odd began to happen to him.
His eyelids began to flutter.
His fingers began to twitch.
He began to stagger.
Suddenly, his body went stiff.
His eyes went blank.
He could not see where he was going!
But Big Ben did not stop.
On and on he went.
On and on, down the twisting path.
On and on, down to the still, green pool.
Big Ben's eyelids shut together with a snap.
He was fast asleep.

At the bottom of the path, the filthy green pool was ready for him.
The Glen of Gloom had him in its wicked grip. Before long, Big Ben was standing on the slippery banks of the pool.
Just one more step and he would sink for ever. But still he did not stop.
Stepping out again, his foot began to come down on the filthy, green scum resting on top of the pool.
Then

'Stop Ben, stop!' called Windbag.

Big Ben stopped.
He shook himself.
Looking down at the pool, he felt sick and dizzy. He was very lucky.
Thank goodness that Windbag had called out to him!
'Thank you, Windbag,' he called out.
'I will come back soon.
I must have a little rest first.'
He still felt giddy, so he sat down on a rock.

But the Glen of Gloom was not ready to let him go just yet.
The green scum on top of the pool was bubbling and oozing.
Before long, it began to froth and splash.
Next, a thick, yellow mist drifted across the glen.
This mist was flooding out of the black cave.
A sickly stink began to fill the glen.
Then

Hiss ... ss .... ss!

Something very big and very, very bad was slithering out of the cave.
Two horrid, blood-red eyes were glittering out of the sooty blackness.
The two eyes were looking at Ben.

B
Big Ben

These eyes were red with anger.
They did not blink.
They did not flicker.
They had no pity.
They were the eyes of a hunter.
They were the eyes of a killer.
They were grim, wicked and crafty.
Big Ben felt a shudder run up and down his back.
His flesh began to creep.
His hands shook.
His legs were as wobbly as a jelly.
But at long last he let out a yell.
'Run Windbag!' he called.
'Run as fast as you can!'

The two fuzzbuzzes went shooting up the crooked path.
The jagged rocks could not stop them.
They were running very, very fast.
The prickly bushes could not stop them.
The two fuzzbuzzes went past them in a flash.
Up and up the path they ran.
Nothing could stop them now.
At last, puffing and panting, they got to the top.

Here, the rest of the clan stood ready to help them.
Ben and Windbag fell down on the grass.
Before long Big Ben was telling them of all the horrid things they had met down in the Glen of Gloom.
Everyone began to chatter.
In the end, Black Angus stood up.
All the chattering stopped.

Wagging his finger at Big Ben and Windbag,
Black Angus said, 'You are silly fools.
Why did you have to go down there?
What a foolish thing to do!
This is not the end.
That thing will come after us.
It will hunt us down.
It will never give up.
It will not stop looking for us until it has us all in its grip.
Because of you we will all suffer.
This is just the beginning.'

With their backs to the horrid glen, the clan set off for the Glen Macfuzz.
Nobody felt happy.
They were all thinking of the thing in the cave.
At long last they got back to the Glen Macfuzz.
Without a word, they crept into the shelter of their little crofts.

Sitting down in his room, Macfuzz the buzz began to think.
What was the thing in the cave?
Was it a wicked monster?
Would it hunt them down?
Could it catch them?
What would it do to them if it did?
Macfuzz the buzz began to shiver.
Out in the blackness of the Glen Macfuzz, everything was very still.

Now write. Do not forget where to put full stops and capital letters.

1 Why did Hilda get angry with Big Ben? (3)
2 What was Jock doing in his garden? (5)
3 Why did Ben carry the picnic hamper? (7)
4 What was in the picnic hamper? (9)
5 What words were cut into the bottom of the big rock? (15)
6 What did the prickly bushes do to Windbag's bonnet? (21)
7 How did Windbag stop Ben from stepping into the green pool? (27)
8 What colour was the mist that drifted out of the cave? (30)
9 Draw the Glen of Gloom and colour it in.
10 What was in the cave?
Draw what *you* think it could be.
Draw how you think it would look.
11 What bit of 'The trip' did you think was the best?